IMAGES
of America

BAXTER STATE PARK
AND KATAHDIN

In 2002, surveyors from the James W. Sewall Company of Old Town, Maine, took this aerial picture of Katahdin. South Peak and the summit are the high points to the left, followed by the jagged teeth of the Knife Edge, Pamola Peak, the Great Basin, Hamlin Peak, and the North Basin. (Courtesy James W. Sewall Company.)

ON THE COVER: These four hikers ascend the precipitous, unstable Abol Slide avalanche, the shortest trail to Katahdin's 4,000-foot-high Tableland. Of note is the climbing attire of the early 20th century. The picture was taken by Albert "Bert" Call, a gifted photographer from Dexter, Maine, who spent years recording wilderness areas of the north woods. (Courtesy Special Collections Department, Raymond H. Fogler Library, University of Maine, Bert Call Collection.)

IMAGES
of America

BAXTER STATE PARK
AND KATAHDIN

John W. Neff and Howard R. Whitcomb

ARCADIA
PUBLISHING

Published by Arcadia Publishing
Charleston, South Carolina

Printed in the United States of America

Library of Congress Control Number: 2011931943

For all general information, please contact Arcadia Publishing:
Telephone 843-853-2070
Fax 843-853-0044
E-mail sales@arcadiapublishing.com
For customer service and orders:
Toll-Free 1-888-313-2665

Visit us on the Internet at www.arcadiapublishing.com

This is the 1941 Geodetic Survey marker at Katahdin's summit. The US National Geodetic Survey (formerly the US Coast and Geodetic Survey) is a constituent part of the National Oceanic and Atmospheric Administration (NOAA) and manages a national coordinate system for mapping and charting. (Courtesy William Bentley.)

CONTENTS

ACKNOWLEDGMENTS

Friends of Baxter State Park is honored to have been asked by Arcadia Publishing to undertake this photographic history of the park and the beloved mountain at its heart. Pres. Barbara Bentley and the board of directors enthusiastically endorsed the project. A steering committee within Friends, consisting of William Bentley, Edward "Zip" Kellogg, and Jym St. Pierre, made helpful editorial and source suggestions. William Bentley expertly scanned images and prepared them for transmission to the publisher. Without Bill's extraordinary assistance, this project would have been infinitely more difficult to complete. We also wish to acknowledge the assistance of Stan Tag, whose proofreading skills were invaluable in the latter stages of this project.

Our research required travel to numerous archives, ranging geographically from Bangor, Millinocket, and Patten in northern Maine, to Boston and Cambridge to the south. We wish to express our appreciation to those who prepared for our visits, responded to our many questions, and were eager to share images in their possession. The catalog of these organizations is impressive and includes Acadia National Park, Appalachian Mountain Club, Bangor Public Library, Baxter State Park, Harvard University Botany Libraries, Maine Appalachian Trail Club, Maine Folklife Center at University of Maine, Maine Historic Preservation Commission, Maine Historical Society, Maine State Archives, Maine State Library, Patten Lumbermen's Museum, the Penobscot Nation at Indian Island, Potomac Appalachian Trail Club, Raymond H. Fogler Library at University of Maine, James W. Sewall Company, and the Thoreau Society.

We also visited or corresponded with many individuals who held personal photographic collections, and we wish to acknowledge them for their generosity in allowing us to use some of their images: Phyllis Austin, William Bentley, Edward Dwyer, Donn Fendler, Gordon Hall, Holly Hamilton, Thomas Hilton, Charlotte Hall Kirkpatrick, Cynthia Knaut, Valerie Knaut, John Neff, and Tony York.

Finally, we want to thank our wives, Helen Neff and Annie Merrill, for their editorial critiques and enthusiastic support as we explored the rich history of Baxter State Park and Katahdin, a subject dear to our hearts.

—John W. Neff, of Winthrop, Maine, and
Howard R. Whitcomb, of Georgetown, Maine

INTRODUCTION

The story of Baxter State Park and the remarkable mountain at its heart begins when the massive continental ice sheet that covered New England 20,000 years ago finally receded. Over the ensuing years, the powerful action of the melting ice left a striking array of glacial cirques, mountain summits, precipitous ridges, high-elevation lakes and ponds, sheer granite walls, basins strewn with rock rubble, and valleys of incomparable beauty carved by glaciers and roaring brooks. Towering above it all was an immense mountain massif. The first people to settle the region millennia after the ice disappeared called it Ktaadn, meaning "greatest mountain." Today, we call it Katahdin.

The mountain is not especially high. At less than a mile above sea level, it is only the sixth highest in all of New England. There is no obvious summit to be observed from below. Rather, there is only a jumbled mass of granite leading to other peaks along the nearby ridges. However, the park's geology, though profoundly interesting, cannot fully explain the special role the mountain and its environs serves in the hearts and minds of all who visit or dream of going there. There has to be something more.

Nor can the special role of the park and mountain be explained by its location. Remote and far removed from urban centers, until the early 19th century, Katahdin was left alone by native people as sacred and bypassed by early surveyors and adventurers as a foreboding wilderness. It was not even climbed for the first time by a nonnative until 1804, a full 162 years after Darby Field clamored to the summit of Mount Washington in 1642. Shortly after the first ascent of Katahdin, geographic surveys began, both before and after Maine statehood in 1820.

The region was then bruised for a century by efforts to extract valuable timber from its slopes and valleys. Yet, the wilderness was never entirely tamed. By the time Katahdin and the future wilderness park that protects it became more accessible in the 20th century, it had already been identified as worthy of being left alone—to be "forever wild." Still, location cannot quite express the mystical attraction of the mountain and the park to those who have been seduced by their bewitching charms.

There is indeed something that more fully reveals the extraordinary lure of Baxter State Park and Katahdin. That is the remarkable human and cultural history of the area. There are rich and engaging stories to be told in every period of the life of the region, and these are the stories told in this photographic essay: There are the deeply moving tales of the native peoples who first drew near to the great mountain massif that arises in such a solitary fashion from the surrounding plains; there are the accounts of hardship and success during scientific explorations and surveys in the early years of the 19th century; one cannot resist the stirring chronicles of explorers, adventurers, and dreamers who wandered over these mountains and valleys eager to discover their secrets; we will "see" the arrival of those who were attracted to climb and camp in the shadow of Katahdin for the pure joy of a wilderness experience and to explore out of curiosity these remote, largely unvisited regions; there is the robust and spirited era of logging in the shadow of Katahdin; we will observe the saga of Gov. Percival P. Baxter's magnificent obsession to preserve and protect the region for all the people; and finally, we will follow the story of the unique park that emerged from that 20th-century grand achievement.

Along the way, we will meet many interesting heroes whose lives will always be intertwined with the region's history—Roy Dudley, Frederic E. Church, Justice William O. Douglas, "Bambi" and one of his creators Maurice "Jake" Day, Donn Fendler, Percival P. Baxter, the Reverend Marcus Keep, Myron Avery, Henry David Thoreau, Fannie Hardy Eckstorm, and a host of others.

This human and cultural history is what makes Baxter State Park and Katahdin such a distinctive and notable place in the hearts of those who journey there and stay long enough to be taken in by its charms.

The native people of Maine have long held a deep, abiding reverence for Katahdin. They sense powerful forces when in the presence of the mountain. They have come to believe in a profoundly personal way that this was the home of the Great Spirit, the creator of the natural world, the one who infuses all of creation with a sustaining presence. Katahdin was and continues to be a sacred place, a place to be approached only with a sense of awe and wonder. Even today, some native people are reluctant to climb the mountain lest the mountain spirits be offended. A lasting legacy of Maine's native people is their stirring stories about the mountain's history. They include the benevolent god Katahdin, the irascible deity Pamola, the hero Gluskabe, and the Spirit of the Night Wind Wuchoswen. This is where Mother Earth reaches out to the sky, a place where the Great Spirit roams freely and powerfully.

Many across the world and through the centuries have felt the same way about other mountains. Edwin Bernbaum writes in his book *Sacred Mountains of the World*:

> The highest and most dramatic features of the natural landscape . . . have an extraordinary power to evoke the sacred. The ethereal rise of a ridge in mist, the glint of moonlight on an icy face, a flare of gold on a distant peak—such glimpses of transcendent beauty can reveal our world as a place of unimaginable mystery and splendor. (San Francisco: Sierra Club Books, 1990, xiii.)

Significantly, Bernbaum includes Katahdin in his list of sacred mountains.

The natives are not alone in their view that this mountain and the surrounding area lure the visitor with a sense of the sacred. Others are guided today toward inner contemplation of the vital center of life in the presence of the mountain. They are like pilgrims seeking the elemental heartbeat or pulse of the spirit. Such is the gift of the native peoples to all who honor this incomparable place set apart to be forever wild.

The earliest known nonnative visitors to the Katahdin region included Joseph Chadwick, who arrived in 1764 while exploring the possibility of a land route between the coast of Maine and the St. Lawrence River. Chadwick returned from Quebec via the West Branch of the Penobscot River that flows just to the south of Katahdin. Other early surveyors, explorers, traders, missionaries, soldiers, and sojourners also may have passed along the same riverine highway close to the towering mountain.

The first recorded ascent of Katahdin was in 1804 when surveyor Charles Turner Jr. and his team climbed along the Southwest Spur (today's Hunt Trail) to the great plateau leading to the summit. In his account, Turner triumphantly reports leaving at the top the party's names scratched on a sheet of lead along with a bottle of rum. Soon after this feat, a great avalanche, today named Abol Slide, came down with a mighty roar on the same southwest side of the mountain in 1816. For many years afterward, the slide was the preferred route to the summit from the Penobscot West Branch.

On March 15, 1820, Maine separated from Massachusetts and became a state. Surveys followed, including an east-west monument line stretching between the provinces of New Brunswick and Quebec in Canada. The line passed over very difficult terrain near Katahdin that caused the line's completion to be delayed for some time. As the years of the 19th century unfolded, a number of scientific explorations were mounted to record geological and botanical observations and to explore the still unvisited areas of the region. Notable among the leaders were Moses Greenleaf, George C. Norris Sr., the Reverend Joseph Blake, Charles T. Jackson, Dr. Aaron Young Jr., Charles Hamlin, and George H. Witherle.

It was not long before those who simply wanted to visit the mountain and the surrounding terrain for their own personal delight and enlightenment organized expeditions to the region. Many came to enhance their understanding of the earth's wild places and to report their findings to others. Two of those deserve special mention. Beginning in 1846, the Reverend Marcus Keep began to visit regularly the new logging roads and trails that led to matchless Katahdin Lake and the East Spur ridgeline leading to Katahdin. He blazed the first formal trail, the Keep Path, to the mountain's tree line and guided visitors into the wilds of the Wassataquoik Valley for more than 30 years. Also noteworthy is Henry David Thoreau's climb toward the summit from the Penobscot West Branch in 1846. He found Katahdin "vast" and "titanic," a place of powerful and mysterious forces. Thoreau left for home having "looked with awe at the ground I trod on." His experience that day made a profound and lasting impression on his life and his literary works. It led him to issue one of the first calls for preserves "where no villages need be destroyed, in which the bear and panther, and some even of the hunter race, may still exist, and not be 'civilized off the face of the earth.' "

Others who came searching for the same ecstatic gratification included the famed Hudson River School painter Frederic E. Church, a young Harvard student and future president named Theodore Roosevelt, folklorist Fannie Hardy Eckstorm, and pioneering members of the renowned Appalachian Mountain Club. They spawned the blazing of early trails as well as the founding of wilderness sporting camps to accommodate the increasing flow of enterprising trekkers.

In the midst of these diverse adventures were those who sensed the wealth to be extracted from the virgin timber they saw from a distance below Katahdin's tree line. The loggers arrived first crossing the East Branch of the Penobscot and ascended the valley of Wassataquoik Stream to cut down dense forest tracts to the north and east of the mountain. Later, the south and southwest sides of the mountain along the tributaries of the West Branch of the Penobscot were logged. In both cases, the logs were at first floated down streams and rivers to the hungry, waiting mills in Bangor. Still later, the logs were intercepted at gigantic pulp and paper mills erected at Millinocket and East Millinocket just above where the two river branches met.

This was a rollicking era for the region: crib dams were built to provide water for the spring river drives, the landscape was scarred and barren from clear cutting and fires, lives were sacrificed to get the logs downstream, fortunes were made and lost, and lumber camps and farms were built to support and feed the men and animals who worked the woods.

If the 19th century belonged to the explorers, the pioneers, the scientists, the loggers, and the recreational climbers, the 20th century belonged to those who had the vision to protect this awe-inspiring realm for future generations and to create an exemplary park to manage it.

Percival Proctor Baxter first saw Katahdin in 1903 when he accompanied his father on a fishing trip to a sporting camp at Kidney Pond. Over the course of the next decade and a half, the future governor devoted himself to family business matters and service in the state legislature. During the 1917–1918 legislative session, his vision of a state park at Katahdin began to take shape. He envisioned the state acquiring the lands surrounding the massif to commemorate the centennial of Maine's 1820 statehood. In 1920, he was a member of an expedition to Katahdin that indelibly affected the remainder of his life. The following January, as a state senator from Cumberland County and president of the Maine Senate, Baxter introduced legislation to create such a park. In a speech delivered before the Maine Sportsmen's Fish and Game Association he stated:

> The proposed park covers an area of 57,232 acres and comprises the whole of Mount Katahdin and Katahdin Lake, of itself one of the most beautiful of all Maine's lakes. . . . The park will bring health and recreation to those who journey there, and the wild life of the woods will find refuge from their pursuers, for the park will be made a bird and game sanctuary for the protection of its forest inhabitants. (*Mount Katahdin State Park*, January 27, 1921, page 13.)

However, the unexpected death of Gov. Frederick H. Parkhurst on January 31, 1921, triggered Baxter's elevation to the governorship. This unforeseen development dramatically changed the political fortunes of his park proposal. As governor, Baxter was unable to secure legislative approval, and the centennial park proposal died.

After leaving the governor's office in 1925, Baxter decided his life's work would be dedicated to the establishment of a park that would guarantee protection of the Katahdin region. Beginning in the early 1930s, he embarked on a three-decade quest to purchase with his own family money and give to the people of Maine 28 parcels of land, which constituted the 201,000-acre Baxter State Park by the time of his death in 1969.

Governor Baxter's deed of March 3, 1931, gifting the 5,960-acre parcel embracing major portions of the Katahdin massif included the following expression of his intent:

> Said premises shall forever be used for public park and recreational purposes, shall forever be left in the natural wild state, shall forever be kept as a sanctuary for wild beasts and birds, that no roads or ways for motor vehicles shall hereafter ever be constructed therein or thereon, and that the grantor, during his lifetime, retains the right to determine, and to place whatever markers or inscriptions shall be maintained or erected on or within the area hereby conveyed. (Private and Special Laws of 1931 [Maine], Chapter 23.)

After the park's establishment in 1933, the state assumed responsibility for managing the new entity. It was tough going at first because of a persistent lack of state funding, the threat of a congressional measure to create a Katahdin National Park, and the challenges of World War II. Gradually, however, thanks to an independent governing authority, a growing commitment by the public, a succession of dedicated rangers and park administrators, and eventually, the proceeds from an endowment fund created by Baxter, the park began to develop a satisfactory trail system and a number of appealing campgrounds. Backcountry areas were opened up to low-key public use, and the northern end of the park was given increased attention. The park has continued to mature in its mission to keep these revered lands, in Baxter's words, "forever wild" while remaining available to visitors yearning for a sense of peace and an opportunity for restoration away from the anxieties and stresses of hectic modern life.

We now invite you to take this photographic journey with us to observe the essence of the park and the iconic mountain that is its heart and soul.

One

EARLY EXPLORERS, ADVENTURERS, AND DREAMERS

The West and East Branches of the Penobscot River flow out of Maine's vast north woods, take slightly different courses, and finally join as one at a place named Nicatou (modern Medway). There, the river begins its journey to the sea, flowing into Penobscot Bay in the Gulf of Maine. Katahdin and the future park surrounding it are located inland from the fork of those two great river branches, both of which played significant roles in the history of the region. The earliest explorers used the West Branch as the highway to approach the mountain. Later, the completion of the Military Road to northern Maine ensured that visitors and loggers seeking to reach the mountain could do so from the East Branch. The extensive east side Wassataquoik Stream watershed played an important role in getting the timber out of the forest and to the mills downriver at the edge of the sea. Access from the West Branch side was then all but abandoned until the 20th century.

In the 19th century, after the nation's birth, northern Maine was New England's greatest remaining frontier. Explorers, surveyors, scientists, and an engaging assortment of adventurers came to learn all they could about this relatively inaccessible territory. The region gradually yielded its secrets, and the development of photography in the mid-1800s ensured that some of the images of those adventures would be recorded. All who ventured there discovered a place of wonder and mystery, and the seeds for preservation were planted. Henry David Thoreau's visits to Maine's north woods in the 1840s and 1850s, including a climb just shy of Katahdin's summit, brought attention to the extraordinary challenges of travel in this wild forest region as well as its riches. He experienced Katahdin as "primeval, untamed, and forever untamable *Nature* . . . something savage and awful, though beautiful." Soon after these adventures, he published an account of the 1846 trip under the title, "Ktaadn and the Maine Woods." At the outset of the 20th century, a young man and future governor, Percival P. Baxter, paid a visit to Kidney Pond in 1903. That visit and the events in his life that followed changed the fate of the Katahdin region profoundly.

Before the arrival of Europeans, the wilderness realm of Maine's north woods belonged to the native peoples who built trails and paddled the rivers and streams to travel from place to place. Here along the Penobscot West Branch, they passed near their sacred mountain Ktaadn. (Courtesy Bangor Public Library, Stodder Collection.)

After the advent of cutting timber in the Katahdin region, Maine's native peoples continued to utilize the waterways for travel. Here, the Indian canoes are alongside the logger's bateau at Ambajejus Lake. The lake was part of a system of waterways to aid the movement of logs downriver. (Courtesy Bangor Public Library, Stodder Collection.)

Joe Attean, an early governor of the Penobscot Nation at Indian Island, Old Town, Maine, is pictured here in formal attire. Attean, known for his intimate knowledge of the north woods and its river passageways, guided Henry David Thoreau in his second expedition to Maine in 1853. (Courtesy Maine Folklife Center, University of Maine.)

When billowing clouds and mist form along the precipitous Knife Edge that connects Katahdin's summit with Pamola Peak, it is thought to be a sign that the mountain spirit is irritated by the presence of strangers entering his realm. Here, the plumes of Pamola are viewed from the summit. (Courtesy John W. Neff.)

MOUNT KTAADN from W. BUTTERFIELD'S (Oct 8th 1836.)
Near the GRAND SCHOODIC LAKE.

Before Maine statehood in 1820, surveyors approached Katahdin to study its unique features. In 1836, Maine's first state geologist, Charles T. Jackson, was commissioned to formally survey state public lands. This drawing, later colored for lithography, shows Katahdin from William Butterfield's farm near Danforth, Maine. In 1837, the survey team reached and climbed Katahdin. The lithograph is by Franz Graeter. (Courtesy Maine State Library.)

After statehood, Maine formed a boundary commission for further land surveys. A base monument line between the Canadian provinces of New Brunswick and Quebec was marked. The line crossed difficult terrain near Katahdin. This 1835 marker in the remote Northwest Basin of Baxter State Park was discovered and photographed in the 1930s. (Courtesy Appalachian Mountain Club Library and Archives.)

Between 1880 and 1901, George H. Witherle made 11 trips to the Katahdin region to explore yet unvisited areas. Sometimes, he teamed with Harvard geologist Charles W. Hamlin to unlock the treasures of this remote territory. At this campsite below Abol Slide, Witherle is at the right; guide George McKenney is at the left. (Courtesy Maine Appalachian Trail Club, Avery Scrapbook.)

Here, George Witherle is on Katahdin's Tableland with other members of his party. Witherle became a member of Boston's Appalachian Mountain Club in 1883 and, along with Charles Hamlin, likely influenced the club's interest in traveling to the remote region beginning in 1886. (Courtesy Maine Appalachian Trail Club, Avery Scrapbook.)

Until the 1800s, early explorers reached Katahdin by canoe along the Penobscot West Branch. From an ancient Indian campsite at the mouth of Abol Stream, climbers (including Thoreau in 1846) ascended toward the summit. The photograph shows the outflow from Nesowadnehunk Falls upriver from the campsite with Katahdin in the distance. (Courtesy Acadia National Park, William Otis Sawtelle Center.)

Lucius Merrill, professor of geology and chemistry at the University of Maine, traveled to the Katahdin region in the 1890s. His photographs provide glimpses of that earlier time in the shadow of the mountain. His rough campsite at Chimney Pond in the South Basin is seen here with the steep glacial headwall behind it. (Courtesy Bangor Public Library, Merrill Collection.)

In the 1830s, access to Katahdin shifted to the eastern side. Taken from Ash Hill in Patten, this photograph shows the territory traversed by early loggers to reach valuable timber below the tree line. They were followed by adventurers who crossed the Penobscot East Branch to reach Katahdin's East Spur (Helon Taylor Trail today). (Courtesy Patten Lumbermen's Museum.)

Hunt Farm, built by pioneer William H. Hunt in the early 1830s, served the loggers who needed to ford the Penobscot East Branch to reach the lumber camps. Soon, he was serving climbers and paddlers who arrived on personal mountain treks. This was the last place of comfort before the rigors of primitive backpacking. (Courtesy Bangor Public Library, Merrill Collection.)

As the loggers moved up Wassataquoik Stream to reach the valley's timber stands, lumber camps were built to support the men and the animals working in the woods. This is Halfway Camp, roughly halfway between Hunt Farm and the extensive Old City Camp farther up the valley. (Courtesy Special Collections Department, Raymond H. Fogler Library, University of Maine, Bert Call Collection.)

By the 1840s, logging had reached Katahdin Lake, west of Wassataquoik Stream. The lake was eventually encircled by logging roads and camps even into the 21st century when logging waned, enabling the forest to begin its long march to recovery. Here, loggers are working at the lake's outlet. (Courtesy Special Collections Department, Raymond H. Fogler Library, University of Maine, Bert Call Collection.)

This is the view that greeted the Reverend Marcus Keep in the summer of 1846 when he reached Katahdin Lake on his way to Katahdin for the first time. Later, Keep and his friends blazed the first formal trail to Katahdin (the Keep Path). The view has changed little through the years. The photograph was taken by Samuel Merrill in 1909. (Courtesy Maine State Library, Avery Collection.)

The Katahdin Lake Camps were founded on the lake's southern shore in the late 1880s by John F. Cushman and Madison M. Tracy to accommodate the increasing number of recreational hikers and climbers. Earlier in 1879, Theodore Roosevelt, along with William "Bill" Wingate Sewell and Wilmont Dow, of Island Falls, camped at the far northern end of Katahdin Lake on their trip to Katahdin. (Courtesy, Maine State Library, Avery Collection.)

This is author Fannie Hardy Eckstorm (1865–1946), whose wide interests included natural history, Maine lumbering history, native folklore, and folk songs of Maine. She roamed the north woods and Katahdin with her fur-trader father and is especially known for her fairness in dealing with Native American contributions to Maine history. (Courtesy Maine Folklife Center, University of Maine.)

Abol Stream flows down Katahdin's southwestern flank and empties here into the Penobscot West Branch. Many early explorers and surveyors of the Katahdin region camped here before their overland journey to the summit. Abol is the short form of the native word *Aboljacknegesic*, meaning "no trees, all smooth." (Courtesy Collections of Maine Historical Society, Maine Memory Network.)

MT. KATAHDIN FROM THE MOUTH OF ABOL ON THE PENOBSCOT WEST BRANCH.

This photograph was taken by James C. Stodder during his trip down the Penobscot West Branch in 1874. Along with a number of canoes, there is one long, narrow bateau. A noted photographer from Bangor, Maine, Stodder created on this trip a classic collection of early photography under very primitive conditions. (Courtesy Bangor Public Library.)

The famed painter of the Hudson River School, Frederic E. Church made many trips to the Katahdin area beginning in 1852 and continuing until his death in 1900. Some of his most acclaimed paintings were of Katahdin, including several painted from the veranda of the cabin he built in 1878 at Millinocket Lake. This image of the massif is from Katahdin Lake. (From *Scribner's Monthly*, May 1878.)

Beloved naturalist and author Henry David Thoreau visited the Katahdin area in 1846 by coming up the Penobscot West Branch in a bateau and camping at the mouth of Abol Stream. The following day, he and his companions climbed toward the summit, encountering swirling mist and strong winds. His experience profoundly influenced his writings. (Courtesy the Thoreau Society Collection at the Thoreau Institute at Walden Woods, Lincoln, Massachusetts.)

At Governor Baxter's instruction, this tablet was placed at a spring located on Katahdin's high Tableland in 1933. The inscription reads, "Henry David Thoreau. 1817–1862. Philosopher. Naturalist. Author. Ascended Mt. Katahdin in 1846 and wrote 'The Maine Woods.' One of the earliest authentic descriptions of the great forest regions of northern Maine." The tablet is no longer extant. (Courtesy Baxter State Park.)

Renowned as the most unique feature of the Katahdin massif, the Knife Edge is a narrow one-mile ridgeline between the summit and Pamola Peak. In this 1900 photograph, a group has traversed the most precipitous part of the ridge and is approaching South Peak. Climbers must always be aware of weather conditions before crossing the ridge. (Courtesy Maine Historic Preservation Commission.)

Shown here is a group of climbers resting along the boulder-strewn Avalanche Brook. The first formal trail to Katahdin, the Keep Path, followed along the banks of this brook before ascending an avalanche to what is now the Keep Ridge just below Pamola Peak and the Knife Edge. Houlton photographer John Bryson took this photograph in 1870. (Courtesy Maine Historic Preservation Commission.)

Hunt Farm on the Penobscot East Branch was located at a ford that enabled loggers and visitors to cross the river comfortably. Here, a horse and buggy takes an Appalachian Mountain Club (AMC) group across on the way to the encampment at Chimney Pond in 1886. Rose Hollingsworth was the photographer for this excursion. (Courtesy Appalachian Mountain Club Library and Archives.)

The old logging road along the north bank of Wassataquoik Stream carried loggers and their supplies to the lumber camps upstream for most of the 19th century. As lumber operations later waned, the road became more and more difficult to negotiate, especially by horse and buggy. This is another Rose Hollingsworth photograph from the 1886 AMC expedition. (Courtesy Appalachian Mountain Club Library and Archives.)

Groups from Boston's Appalachian Mountain Club first came into the Katahdin region in 1886 and returned off and on for many years afterward. Here is a 1920 AMC campsite at Chimney Pond in the Great Basin. Club members spent much of their time building trails and erecting signs to aid other climbers. (Courtesy Appalachian Mountain Club Library and Archives.)

Moose are a common sight in Baxter State Park. Here, a cow and her calf share a moment while feeding at Sandy Stream Pond near Roaring Brook Campground. Picture Rock on the shore of the pond is a favorite place to view the Katahdin massif and the nearby browsing moose. (Courtesy John W. Neff.)

The Great Northern Paper Company began to cut timber in the near-tree-line Basin Ponds area in the 1920s. There, this large lumber camp was built to support the short-lived effort. Of note is the clear-cut area with the Blueberry Knoll and Hamlin Ridge in the background. (Courtesy Special Collections Department, Raymond H. Fogler Library, University of Maine, Bert Call Collection.)

Edward B. Draper managed the Katahdin Pulp and Paper Company, which, in 1910, began salvaging timber that survived the great Wassataquoik Valley fire in 1903. Later, logging moved farther up the valley. Here, a logger is yarding logs in the Northwest Basin. The basin's precipitous headwall appears in the background. (Courtesy Maine Appalachian Trail Club, Avery Scrapbook.)

It is winter at the Pogy Brook Lumber Camp in Baxter State Park's interior north of Russell Pond. The camps were very isolated in the winter when most of the logging took place in preparation for the spring river drives. The man with the apron is likely the "cookie" for the group. (Courtesy Maine State Library, Avery Collection.)

Before a fire in 1915 halted lumbering on South Pogy Mountain, a logging operation took place on its higher elevations. A steep sluice sent logs down into Wassataquoik Lake where they remained until the spring drive. The logs gathered so much momentum they literally exploded off the sluice onto the frozen lake. (Courtesy Maine State Library, Avery Collection.)

George Annis, boss of lumber operations in the upper Wassataquoik Valley, stands in front of a camp building. He gave his name to Annis Brook, which flows off the slopes of Fort and Mullen Mountains in the range of hills named the Katahdinauguoh. Today's Northwest Basin Trail passes through this area. (Courtesy Maine Appalachian Trail Club, Avery Scrapbook.)

As the rock inscription reveals, Foster Tracy and Hugh Love began lumbering the Wassataquoik Valley in 1883. It was an immense operation, requiring many dams to store water to help logs avoid boulders blocking the stream. The huge Mammoth Dam appears behind the rock. The photograph is by George H. Hallowell. (Courtesy Maine State Library, Avery Collection.)

The logging camps around Katahdin were austere but provided the loggers a safe place during long winter operations. Here is the inside of the Ledge Falls Camp along Nesowadnehunk Stream in 1892. Of note are the clothes hanging up to dry. Today, Ledge Falls is a favorite picnic stop along the park's Tote Road. (Courtesy Patten Lumbermen's Museum.)

Here, a group of nine loggers has stopped in front of a giant boulder to enjoy their dinner. They are in the Wassataquoik Stream Valley and no doubt are tired from working in the woods. Of note is the giant peavey used to work the logjams that often hindered the flow of logs on the river. This photograph is by Lore A. Rogers. (Courtesy Patten Lumbermen's Museum.)

When logging began in the Wassataquoik Valley, small lumber camps were built as the operations advanced. Later, a major camp was needed to support the men and animals working the woods. Here are two buildings at what came to be known as Old City Camp below Grand Falls. (Courtesy Bangor Public Library, Merrill Collection.)

Here is a group of loggers taking a break for a photograph. Of note is the wide array of peaveys, pickeroons, and poles used to keep the logs rolling along during the stream and river drives. It was very dangerous work and called for a high level of daring and courage. (Courtesy Maine Appalachian Trail Club, Avery Scrapbook.)

This rare photograph shows lumbering operations on Nesowadnehunk Stream. The logs were "twitched" down the stream before passing under a toll dam built in 1880 and into the swirling waters of Little Niagara Falls and Big Niagara Falls below. Both peaks of Doubletop Mountain are visible in the distance. (Courtesy Phyllis Austin.)

After passing through the quiet waters above the Nesowadnehunk Stream toll dam, logs tumbled down Little Niagara Falls and Big Niagara Falls in quick succession. The saying was that one could always tell a "Sourdnahunk" log because it had no bark left by the time it reached the Penobscot West Branch. (Courtesy Phyllis Austin.)

In the 1920s, a French Canadian river driver, unknown even to his companions, drowned in turbulent spring waters while driving logs down Nesowadnehunk Stream. He was buried near the riverbank where the accident occurred. The gravesite was discovered and marked in the 1930s, and the cross and sign can be seen today near Foster Field. (Courtesy Baxter State Park.)

In 1880, the Sourdnahunk Dam and Improvement Company erected a toll dam just above Little Niagara Falls to profit from the flow of logs driven toward the Penobscot West Branch. The charge was 63¢ per 1,000 feet of timber. The remains of the dam are one mile below Daicey Pond. (Courtesy Special Collections Department, Raymond H. Fogler Library, University of Maine, Bert Call Collection.)

The bateau was the workhorse of the river drivers, providing protection while working on a river full of logs and light enough to be shouldered across a waterfall carry. The bateau could also negotiate moderate white water easily. This photograph is by artist George H. Hallowell. (Courtesy Maine Folklife Center, University of Maine.)

Here, loggers attempt to free a logjam hindering the flow of logs on the Penobscot East Branch. They are using peaveys and pickeroons, their feet shod with cleated boots to facilitate using the logs for footholds. Logjams were frequent in the region because of glacial boulders in most of the streams. (Courtesy Maine Folklife Center, University of Maine.)

The Great Northern Paper Company began building its huge pulp and paper mill in Millinocket in 1899. Logs once headed to Old Town near Bangor were diverted to the mill beginning in 1900. In this aerial photograph, snow-capped Katahdin is visible in the distance, and the mill is at the left foreground. (Courtesy Maine State Library, Baxter Collection.)

MOUNT KATAHDIN, FROM GREAT NORTHERN HOTEL, MILLINOCKET, ME.

Katahdin region visitors pass through Millinocket on their way to Baxter State Park and other recreational destinations. The town provides accommodations and supplies for those who will soon experience more primitive conditions in the north woods. This is the view from the venerable Great Northern Hotel that later burned down. (Courtesy Phyllis Austin.)

This c. 1900 photograph by Leyland Whipple shows two spotters at the summit of Katahdin scanning the countryside for possible fires. There were a number of fires in the interior north and east of Katahdin in the late 1800s, and perhaps these men were employed by the state to ensure early detection. (Courtesy Bangor Public Library.)

In 1884, a great fire broke out near Old City Camps in a heavily lumbered area along Wassataquoik Stream. Started by a campfire spark, the fire burned 22,000 acres and forced loggers to cut only burned wood for several years. The photograph, taken near Orin Falls, shows the devastation from that fire. (Courtesy Bangor Public Library, Merrill Collection.)

The photograph shows how complete the devastation was from the Wassataquoik Valley fires in the 1880s and later in 1903. Scars from the fires could readily be seen for many years, but gradually, the forest began to recover. Today, visitors can roam through the valley, seeing little of its destructive past. (Courtesy Appalachian Mountain Club Library and Archives.)

As there was an Old City Lumber Camp, so there was a New City Lumber Camp. The latter was located near the confluence of the Main and South Branches of Wassataquoik Stream. This view with the camp in the distance shows the devastation wrought by heavy lumbering and fires in the early 1900s. (Courtesy Maine State Library, Avery Collection.)

Two

THE JOURNEY TOWARD PROTECTION BEGINS

As the 20th century dawned, sporting camps were established to accommodate those who sought to climb Katahdin or fish and relax in its shadow. Members of the famed Appalachian Mountain Club in Boston began to construct trails and provide signs to guide the hikers. In the 1930s, Maine native Myron H. Avery convinced the newly formed Appalachian Trail Conference to extend the Appalachian Trail (AT) to the summit of Katahdin, and work began in 1933 to white-blaze the AT within the park. A significant portion of the future state park was officially designated the Katahdin Game Preserve, a first step toward protection. In the wings, however, powerful forces were at work to ensure more reliable protection for this wilderness area.

As noted in the Introduction, Percival Baxter's gifts totaling 201,000 acres over three decade ensured the protection of the region surrounding the Katahdin massif. The deeds of trust that accompanied each of the gifts were an expression of Baxter's intent and used to guide the Baxter State Park Authority and park personnel in their management responsibilities.

In 1955, the state legislature formally adopted language suggested by former Governor Baxter that clarified the meaning of the terms "natural wild state" and "sanctuary for wild beasts and birds" that appeared repeatedly in the deeds of trust. Included therein was the foundational statement with its unequivocal language that established the primacy of wilderness over recreational interests in the management of Baxter State Park:

> This area is to be maintained primarily as a Wilderness and recreational purposes are to be regarded as of secondary importance and shall not encroach upon the main objective of this area which is to be "Forever Wild." (Private and Special Laws of 1955 [Maine], Chapter 2.)

Just as Baxter had been determined to ensure that the conditions of the deeds of trust be honored during his lifetime, he was equally assiduous in ensuring that there were sufficient endowment monies to protect the park's future financial independence and, if warranted, permit the acquisition of additional lands.

This photographic history celebrates this remarkable legacy, tells of those who managed the park in its early years, illuminates the arrival of the Appalachian Trail to Katahdin's summit, and gives a glimpse of some of those who made their mark on the park's history.

The Katahdin Lake Camps, now known as the Katahdin Lake Wilderness Camps, were established in the late 1880s. At the time of this early-20th-century photograph, the camps were operated by one of its cofounders John Cushman. Here, Cushman is with his daughter-in-law Lizzie and her son Merle. (Courtesy Holly Hamilton.)

Here, John Cushman's grandson Merle and a childhood friend are seen playing in the midst of the camp's wood supply. Cushman sold the camps in 1919. In 2006, in the aftermath of the park's acquisition of the Katahdin Lake parcel, the Katahdin Lake Wilderness Camps obtained a lease to continue operations at the historic site. (Courtesy Holly Hamilton.)

Nesowadnehunk Stream flows through a valley west of Katahdin and empties into the Penobscot West Branch. Three major sporting camps grew up along its watershed in the 1890s: Camp Phoenix on "Sourdnahunk" Lake, Twin Pine Camps on Daicey Pond, and Kidney Pond Camps. In the winter, the stream belonged to the loggers who piled timber on its banks in preparation for the spring river drives. (Courtesy Patten Lumbermen's Museum.)

Kidney Pond Camps has been a popular facility from the 1890s to the present. A central lodge was surrounded by small cabins for overnight visitors. From the start, the camps provided many comforts of home in a wilderness setting. They still provide shelter and refuge for visitors seeking a place of peace. (Courtesy Maine State Archives.)

Reaching Kidney Pond Camps in the early years involved a train ride from Boston, a canoe paddle up the Penobscot West Branch, and a final push by foot to the camps. Along with guides to hiking and fishing opportunities, three meals and comfortable beds were provided. (Courtesy Special Collections Department, Raymond H. Fogler Library, University of Maine, Bert Call Collection.)

Inside the spacious lodge of Kidney Pond Camps were dining tables, an extensive library, comfortable chairs, and the welcoming glow of a daily fire. Guests gathered there when they felt the need for camaraderie or a break after the rigors of the day. (Courtesy Special Collections Department, Raymond H. Fogler Library, University of Maine, Bert Call Collection.)

Bears in search of food frequented the sporting camps, and visitors were warned not to leave food the bears could reach. The dumps established by the camps were regularly raided by bears. Today, visitors must pack out what they bring into the park, and bears are seldom seen even on the trail. (Courtesy Baxter State Park.)

Many sporting camps maintained large tents on the shores of outlying ponds and streams a half-day hike from the central camps. This tent at Slaughter Pond accommodated guests who wished to have a more primitive experience during their stay. The evening meal often included fish caught in the pond that day. (Courtesy Maine Historic Preservation Commission.)

This is the view from Rocky Pond less than a mile from Kidney Pond Campground. In the view, Doubletop and Moose Mountains can be seen. At campground ranger stations, visitors can rent canoes for day use on outlying ponds. (Courtesy Special Collections Department, Raymond H. Fogler Library, University of Maine, Bert Call Collection.)

Most of the campgrounds in the park are near prime moose-feeding areas, and it is not uncommon for visitors to share their daily routines with moose, which largely ignore the guests unless they get too close. Here, a photographer tries to get as close as possible before snapping the picture. (Courtesy Special Collections Department, Raymond H. Fogler Library, University of Maine, Bert Call Collection.)

The Twin Pine Camps were established by Maurice York on Daicey Pond in 1899, and the camps continued under the ownership of the York family for an unequaled 70 years. The two tall pines have grown considerably and still rule over the site of the park's Daicey Pond Campground. (Courtesy Maine State Library, Avery Collection.)

From the porch of the Twin Pine Camps lodge/library, visitors can see the Hunt Spur leading to Katahdin and the remote, largely unvisited country to the west of the mountain. Out on the pond, several loon families might be seen by day and their haunting cry heard in the night. (Courtesy Collections of Maine Historical Society, Maine Memory Network.)

On the Penobscot East Branch side of Katahdin, the Lunksoos Sporting Camps were established at an old farm site. At one time, the camps maintained this crude ferry to carry hikers across to trails leading to Katahdin Lake and beyond. Portions of the cable that supported the ferry can still be seen at the site. (Courtesy Appalachian Mountain Club Library and Archives.)

Camp Phoenix, a sporting camp on Nesowadnehunk Lake, was established about 1900. Guests arrived from the Penobscot West Branch and also from Patten along the Eastern Corporation's lumber road. Fishing and hunting were the main features of these camps that are now a private community of cabins, each individually owned. (Courtesy Special Collections Department, Raymond H. Fogler Library, University of Maine, Bert Call Collection.)

The lumber camps at Robar's Landing were located along Wassataquoik Stream as logging activity moved up the valley in the late 19th century. It was a bustling place, providing shelter and supplies for the vast timber cutting going on throughout the valley. Israel Robar later lived out his so-called hermit life at the site. (Courtesy Gray Herbarium Library Archives, Harvard University.)

As lumbering moved closer to Katahdin in the late 1880s, McLeod Camp was established along the South Branch of the Wassataquoik. It lasted only a short time but provided needed shelter and supplies for the loggers in that watershed. From there, one of the earliest trails to Katahdin was built toward the North Peaks area. (Courtesy Holly Hamilton.)

In July 1900, five members of the New England Botanical Club undertook an excursion to Katahdin. Here, one of the botanists, Dr. George G. Kennedy, sits in the rough-hewn Camp Kennedy, a single-room structure about 20 feet square, which was built from unpeeled spruce logs harvested on-site at Chimney Pond specifically for the expedition. (Courtesy Gray Herbarium Library Archives, Harvard University.)

In this 1900 photograph, Lore Rogers, of Patten, sits at the guide's lean-to with the exterior of Camp Kennedy at the left rear. Rogers used an old slide near the present Saddle Trail on his first ascent of the mountain in 1887. (Courtesy Maine Appalachian Trail Club, Avery Scrapbook.)

On ledges of basin headwalls, the botanists found "the curious convex tufts of the *Diapensia*, with even surface, but the large white flowers projecting, like pins and ornaments from a pincushion." The results of the expedition, including a fascinating account of the party's itinerary, were published in the June 1901 issue of *Rhodora*. (Courtesy Special Collections Department, Raymond H. Fogler Library, University of Maine, Ralph Palmer Collection.)

Included in this summit photograph of July 11, 1900, are the five botanists: Dr. George G. Kennedy, Merritt L. Fernald (of the Gray Herbarium at Harvard), J. Franklin Collins (of Brown University), Emile F. Williams, and Joseph R. Churchill along with two guides, one of whom is Lore Rogers. (Courtesy Gray Herbarium Library Archives, Harvard University.)

This iconic photograph of Percival Baxter in a bateau crossing the East Branch of the Penobscot River is from the August 1920 expedition to Katahdin designed to promote Baxter's forthcoming proposal for a Mount Katahdin State Park. Arthur G. Staples, at Baxter's left in the bow, wrote a lengthy newspaper account of the expedition. (Courtesy Maine State Library.)

The itinerary of Baxter's 1920 expedition included the southern shore of Katahdin Lake where Cushman's camps had been located. Although W.F. Dawson, who photographed this scene, was not a member of Baxter's expedition, he characterized the camps as "an ideal location for park buildings and headquarters." (Courtesy Maine State Library, Avery Collection.)

This mid-1930s image of the beach at Katahdin Lake gives a sense of what Baxter's party would have seen in 1920. In his account of the 1920 expedition's arrival along the southern shore of Katahdin Lake, Arthur G. Staples described the bleak, serrated top of Katahdin arising beyond the lakeshore. (Courtesy Acadia National Park, William Otis Sawtelle Center.)

There are few extant photographs of Baxter's 1920 expedition. This one shows the expedition's cook J. Howard Ambrose using a reflector oven before the cook fire at Katahdin's South Basin. This site at Chimney Pond served as the expedition's base camp with Baxter ascending Katahdin with Roy Dudley's group via Pamola Peak. (Courtesy Appalachian Mountain Club Library and Archives.)

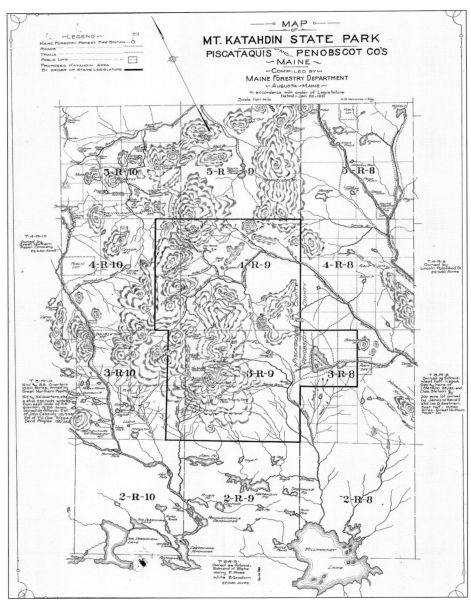

This January 1921 Maine Department of Forestry map was prepared for then-Senator Baxter to accompany his legislative proposal for a Mount Katahdin State Park to commemorate the centennial of Maine's 1820 statehood. The proposed park comprised 57,232 acres, including much of the Katahdin massif and Katahdin Lake six miles east-northeast of the summit. The death of Gov. Frederick H. Parkhurst on January 31 triggered senate president Baxter's elevation to the governorship. This unforeseen development dramatically changed the political fortunes of Baxter's park proposal. Photographer W.F. Dawson's illustrated lecture on the proposed park was canceled, and legislators instead were filing past Parkhurst's coffin in the capitol's rotunda. As governor (1921–1925), Baxter was never able to convince his former legislative colleagues to pass the Mount Katahdin State Park legislation. Nevertheless, Baxter remained resolute that a park should be established at Katahdin. (Courtesy Baxter State Park.)

Percival Baxter maintained a cordial relationship for three decades with Great Northern Paper's vice president William Hilton, who managed its two million acres of northern Maine woodlands. On the occasion of the last title transfer from the company to Baxter in 1962, Baxter said of Hilton, "Without your help there would be no Baxter State Park today." (Courtesy Thomas L. Hilton.)

This tablet at Chimney Pond was erected to commemorate the gift of the initial parcel of 5,960 acres to the state. In the deeds of trust accompanying this gift, Baxter specified that during his lifetime, he retained the right to place "whatever markers or inscriptions . . . on or within the area hereby conveyed." (Courtesy Maine State Library, Avery Collection.)

BAXTER STATE PARK

THE GIFT OF MT. KATAHDIN TO THE STATE OF MAINE BY PERCIVAL PROCTOR BAXTER (GOVERNOR 1921-1925) WAS ACCEPTED BY THE STATE LEGISLATURE REPRESENTING THE PEOPLE OF MAINE BY CHAPTER 3, PRIVATE AND SPECIAL LAWS OF MAINE 1933, APPROVED BY GOVERNOR LOUIS J. BRANN FEBRUARY 9, 1933 "THE SAME TO BE FOREVER HELD BY THE SAID STATE IN TRUST FOR THE PEOPLE OF MAINE FOR STATE FOREST, PUBLIC PARK AND RECREATIONAL PURPOSES," AND UPON THE FURTHER CONDITION THAT THE SAME "SHALL FOREVER BE LEFT IN THE NATURAL WILD STATE, SHALL FOREVER BE KEPT AS A SANCTUARY FOR WILD BEASTS AND BIRDS, THAT NO ROADS OR WAYS FOR MOTOR VEHICLES SHALL HEREAFTER EVER BE CONSTRUCTED THEREON OR THEREIN."

THE STATE LEGISLATURE BY CHAPTER 103 OF THE RESOLVES OF MAINE 1933, APPROVED BY GOVERNOR LOUIS J. BRANN MARCH 23, 1933 PROVIDED THAT THE AREA DONATED AND CONVEYED TO THE STATE AS ABOVE DESCRIBED "IS HEREBY NAMED 'BAXTER STATE PARK' IN HONOR OF THE DONOR, AND THE SAME SHALL HEREAFTER BE SO DESIGNATED ON THE OFFICIAL MAPS AND RECORDS OF THE STATE."

THIS TABLET ERECTED 1936 BY ORDER OF THE GOVERNOR AND EXECUTIVE COUNCIL

GEORGE J. STOBIE
WALDO N. SEAVEY
FREDERICK P. BONNEY
JOHN F. WARD
BAXTER STATE PARK COMMISSIONERS.

GEORGE C. LORD   RAYMOND S. OAKES
FRED L. LEAVITT   CLYDE H. SMITH
ALLEN M. SMALL   ORMAN B. FERNANDEZ   LOUIS J. BRANN
ERNEST A. WOODMAN   EXECUTIVE COUNCILLORS.   GOVERNOR.

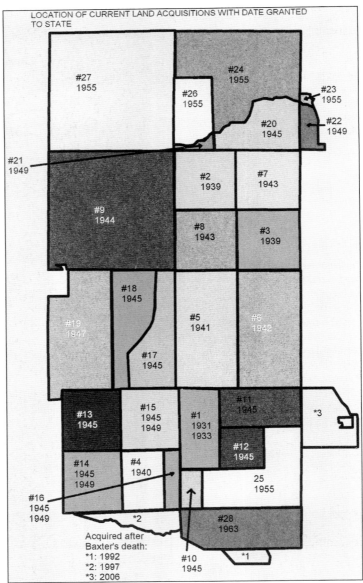

#27
1955

#24
1955

#26
1955

#23
1955

#20
1945

#22
1949

#21
1949

#2
1939

#7
1943

#9
1944

#8
1943

#3
1939

#18
1945

#19
1947

#5
1941

#6
1942

#17
1945

#11
1945

*3

#13
1945

#15
1945
1949

#1
1931
1933

#12
1945

#14
1945
1949

#4
1940

25
1955

#16
1945
1949

*2

#28
1963

Acquired after
Baxter's death:
*1: 1992
*2: 1997
*3: 2006

#10
1945

*1

This map provides the location of Baxter State Park land acquisitions with their respective dates granted to the state of Maine. During Governor Baxter's lifetime, 28 of the parcels were acquired. In 1955, on the occasion of his largest gift of more than 52,000 acres, Baxter wrote to Gov. Edmund S. Muskie, "A map showing the different acquisitions both small and large over the years would remind you of your grandmother's patchwork quilt, which finally in some mysterious way came out of the confusion into one large piece." After Baxter's death in 1969, three additional parcels were added to the park. In 1992 and 1997, two small pieces of land were added along the park's southern boundary, namely, the Togue Pond parcel and the West Branch lands. The park's total acreage after the 2006 Katahdin Lake acquisition was 209,501 acres. Not shown on the map is a 143-acre private parcel on the eastern shore of Katahdin Lake that was transferred to Baxter State Park in January 2012, thereby increasing the park's size to 209,644 deeded acres. (Courtesy Baxter State Park.)

Baxter, a Phi Beta Kappa graduate of Bowdoin College, studied law at Harvard but never practiced. As a young man, he devoted himself to family business matters and service in the state legislature. As governor in the early 1920s, Baxter was best known as a fiscal conservative and an advocate of the state's natural resources. (Courtesy Maine State Library, Baxter Collection.)

This is a Spruce Grouse in a classic pose in its favored habitat. Governor Baxter's initial Deed of Trust in 1931 specified that the park "shall forever be left in the natural wild state, shall forever be kept as a sanctuary for wild beasts and birds." (Courtesy Special Collections Department, Raymond H. Fogler Library, University of Maine, Harold Dyer Collection.)

Helon Taylor, a former state game warden, became park superintendent in 1950. In those post–World War II years, the park flourished under Taylor's management. He enjoyed the strong support of Baxter, and the men had a rich personal friendship. The Helon Taylor Trail from Roaring Brook Campground to Pamola is named in his honor. (Courtesy Maine State Library, Baxter Collection.)

Percival Baxter continued to make inspection visits throughout his latter years. Here, he is seen fly-fishing at Kidney Pond. During his lifetime, Baxter carefully monitored compliance with the deeds of trust but also ensured that there were sufficient endowment monies to protect the park's future independence. (Courtesy Special Collections Department, Raymond H. Fogler Library, University of Maine, Harold Dyer Collection.)

It was difficult getting to Katahdin in 1931. Here, Charlotte Millet and Electa McClain, two residents of Percival P. Baxter's ancestral hometown of Gorham, travel in a horse-drawn wagon along the bank of the Nesowadnehunk Stream. Baxter State Park would be formally established by legislative action in 1933. (Courtesy Collections of Maine Historical Society, Maine Memory Network.)

This image is of a buckboard carrying passengers across the Nesowadnehunk Stream. It required an all-day excursion with multiple modes of transportation before travelers were treated to a sumptuous evening meal and overnight lodging at a neighboring sporting camp, most likely at either Daicey or Kidney Ponds. (Courtesy Baxter State Park.)

As the years progressed, private automobiles began to use logging roads along the western boundary of the park. Here, an automobile is fording the Nesowadnehunk, most likely to take "sports" to the Kidney Pond Camps. Baxter State Park roads remain narrow and unpaved at the wishes of its benefactor. (Courtesy Baxter State Park.)

There was no shortage of wildlife along the streams and ponds of the park. Those traveling by buckboard or automobile would often see moose along the Nesowadnehunk Stream. Maine's boreal forest provides a natural habitat for these marvelous creatures, the largest extant species of the deer family. (Courtesy Baxter State Park.)

Vehicular access on the eastern side of the park was greatly improved in 1935 when the Civilian Conservation Corps upgraded Great Northern's Tote Road to Roaring Brook where a campground would be established in 1950. Here is the gravel road at Windey Pitch on October 18, 1945, with snow already accumulating on Katahdin. (Courtesy Maine State Library, Avery Collection.)

Here, an automobile with 1925 Maine dealer plates navigates among glacial erratics along an old tote road. What is now the Park Tote Road was known as the Perimeter Road for many years. It was renamed to commemorate its original purpose and the loggers who worked in the region. (Courtesy Special Collections Department, Raymond H. Fogler Library, University of Maine, Bert Call Collection.)

On the route from Millinocket to the park there are several landmarks, including a narrow spit of land between Ambajejus and Millinocket Lakes, and this scenic vista of Pockwockamus Rock. The hill above the huge glacial erratic where the vintage car is parked provided the adventurous, even in the 1950s, with a wonderful view of Katahdin. (Courtesy Special Collections Department, Raymond H. Fogler Library, University of Maine, Bert Call Collection.)

From 1928 to 1958, Lester Hall of Nobleboro made almost annual treks to Katahdin, many with his friend Maurice "Jake" Day of Damariscotta. Lester's published journals provide fascinating insights of the early days of the park, both north and south. This is Lester's 1921 Dodge, which proved to be reliable on his early trips to Katahdin. (Courtesy Charlotte Hall Kirkpatrick.)

The completion of a new road from Togue Pond to Abol Campground in the 1960s resulted in this junction at Togue Pond Gatehouse. The right fork is the Roaring Brook Road, whereas the left is the beginning of the Park Tote Road that terminates at the Matagamon Gatehouse in the northeastern corner of the park. (Courtesy Maine State Library, Baxter Collection.)

At Matagamon Lake, the park's gatehouse provides access to the northern end of the park, including the campgrounds at Trout Brook Farm and South Branch Pond. Wonderful trails abound in this area, including the Traveler Loop and the Pogy Notch Trail to the park's interior at Russell Pond. (Courtesy Maine State Library, Baxter Collection.)

In 1925, Gov. Ralph Owen Brewster became the first incumbent governor to climb Katahdin. This photograph from that trip shows Brewster and his wife, Dorothy, at what was then called Monument Peak. The photograph was used in the mid-1930s in promotional materials for Congressman Brewster's proposal to create a national park at Katahdin. The effort failed in the face of adamant opposition from Baxter. (Courtesy Holly Hamilton.)

This chiseled marker at the junction of the Hunt and Abol Trails commemorated Governor Brewster's ascent of Katahdin in 1925. Inland Fisheries and Wildlife commissioner Willis E. Parsons directed its inscription on the granite boulder at the Tableland spring where the Brewster party had lunch on the day of the climb. (Courtesy Special Collections Department, Raymond H. Fogler Library, University of Maine, Bert Call Collection.)

This 1928 photograph of a hiking party picnicking at Governor's Spring reveals both the gradual slope and vastness of the Tableland. The cairn atop the granite boulder is typical of trail markers on the plateau. The site was renamed Thoreau Spring in 1933 at Baxter's request. (Courtesy Special Collections Department, Raymond H. Fogler Library, University of Maine, Bert Call Collection.)

The Department of Interior's National Park Service commissioned extensive photography in the Katahdin region in conjunction with Congressman Brewster's national park proposal. This iconic photograph from 1937, commonly known as the "Holmberg Aerial," shows the main geological features of the Katahdin massif in stunning detail. (Courtesy Baxter State Park.)

The 19th-century Maine Boundary Commission's Monument Line, the base boundary line of the state, gave rise to designations, such as Township 2 Range 10. Here, a survey crewmember paints a boundary marker along the southern border of the park around 1940–1941. (Courtesy Special Collections Department, Raymond H. Fogler Library, University of Maine, Harold Dyer Collection.)

In May 1942, Harold Dyer became the first supervisor of Baxter State Park. He was professionally trained in wildlife management and was known for his prodigious work habits and analytical reports on management and development issues. Here, a snowshoe-clad Dyer takes a breather at a hastily built warming fire. (Courtesy Special Collections Department, Raymond H. Fogler Library, University of Maine, Harold Dyer Collection.)

Irvin "Buzz" Caverly's tenure as a Baxter State Park employee began in 1960 as a seasonal ranger. He retired in 2005 after serving 24 years as park director. During his earliest years at the park, Caverly worked under the tutelage of Governor Baxter, and he would remain faithful to his mentor's wilderness values and vision for the park. (Courtesy Edward Dwyer.)

This gathering of Baxter State Park Authority members James S. Erwin, Ronald R. Speers, and Austin Wilkins (left to right) along with Gov. Kenneth M. Curtis (second from right) is on the occasion of the 1967 dedication of the Togue Pond Gatehouse. Baxter's remarks delivered in absentia were his last regarding "his" beloved park. (Courtesy Maine State Library, Baxter Collection.)

On the left is Benton MacKaye, whose visionary writings in the 1920s resulted in the creation of the Appalachian Trail. On the right is Maine native Myron H. Avery, whose persistence resulted in the setting of the northern terminus of the AT at Katahdin rather than Mount Washington. (Courtesy Potomac Appalachian Trail Club, www.patc.net.)

Here, Myron Avery (center) and his friends Albert H. Jackman (left) and J. Frank Schairer (right) pose on the summit of Katahdin on August 19, 1933, when they began cutting and marking the Appalachian Trail across Maine. The wheel measured the exact mileage of the footpath. The photograph is by Shailer S. Philbrick. (Courtesy Potomac Appalachian Trail Club, www.patc.net.)

At first, AT hikers crossed the Penobscot West Branch south of Katahdin over the Nesowadnehunk Falls dam, but after the dam collapsed, they crossed by canoe or bateau. This cable bridge, built by the CCC in 1936, provided safe crossings until the mid-1950s when the trail was relocated. (Courtesy Maine State Library, Avery Collection.)

Katahdin Stream Falls

The Appalachian Trail crosses Katahdin Stream below a spectacular falls one mile northeast of its namesake campground. The rustic bridge near this final tumble of water gives a foretaste of the treasures farther up the trail as it climbs through forest cover to the open boulder-strewn ridge and plateau beyond. (Courtesy Maine Historic Preservation Commission.)

Myron Avery leads members of the Potomac Appalachian Trail Club from Washington, DC, up through the giant granite boulders of the upper Hunt Trail below the Gateway. Once again, he has his measuring wheel in hand to record the exact distances along the Appalachian Trail. (Courtesy Potomac Appalachian Trail Club, www.patc.net.)

After hikers on the AT have negotiated the huge boulders along the Hunt Spur, they reach the Gateway and start across the vast Tableland to the summit. Here, Emmie Bailey Whitney is seen at the Gateway looking out over the expanse to the southwest. Marking the Gateway are two granite steles. (Courtesy Collections of Maine Historical Society, Maine Memory Network.)

The first trail signs erected in the Katahdin region were provided by Boston's Appalachian Mountain Club. The upper sign, installed by the AMC, is mated with the Appalachian Trail Conference sign providing sporting camp information for AT hikers. Springer Mountain, Georgia, later replaced Mount Ogelthorpe as the southern terminus of the famous trail. (Courtesy Appalachian Mountain Club Library and Archives.)

Ronald Gower (left), a leader in the Appalachian Mountain Club, is replacing the upper section of the summit sign supported by a pile of rocks. Gower journeyed often to the Katahdin region for trail maintenance and trip leadership. (Courtesy Appalachian Mountain Club Library and Archives.)

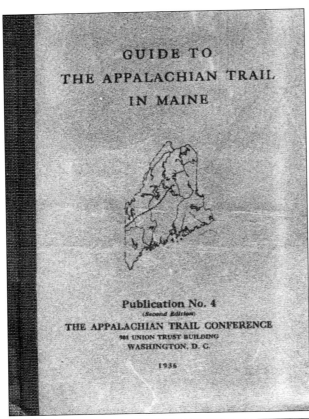

GUIDE TO
THE APPALACHIAN TRAIL
IN MAINE

Publication No. 4
(Second Edition)
THE APPALACHIAN TRAIL CONFERENCE
901 UNION TRUST BUILDING
WASHINGTON, D. C.

1936

The AMC published the first guide to the Katahdin region in 1917 and the first contour map in 1925. The club continued to provide guidebook revisions until the mid-1930s when the Appalachian Trail Conference, and later its trail partner the Maine Appalachian Trail Club, assumed the responsibility for publishing guidebooks on the AT in Maine as well as Baxter State Park. (Courtesy Maine State Library, Avery Collection.)

In August 1939, the Appalachian Trail Conference met at Twin Pine Camps at Daicey Pond to celebrate the AT's extension to Katahdin and the completion of the whole trail from Maine to Georgia. Shown are vintage cars in the open field below the campground where food and meeting tents were erected. (Courtesy Collections of Maine Historical Society, S-Collection. 6196: 178/1.)

Mountain cranberries cover many areas above Katahdin's tree line, enduring the harsh winter conditions admirably. As the Reverend Marcus Keep descended from Pamola Peak in 1847, he stopped to pick berries at the top of the East Slide avalanche. He speculated they were so plentiful that a local business could easily be created. (Courtesy Charlotte Hall Kirkpatrick.)

Katahdin's summit sign is always a welcome sight to hikers nearing the top of the 5,267-feet peak. This c. 1950s sign was later replaced by one on tripod posts to avoid wind damage. Attached to the sign is an old ATC metal cylinder installed to keep the summit register dry. (Courtesy Baxter State Park.)

In the late 1920s, a small lumber camp stood where Katahdin Stream crossed an old tote road. In 1934, the CCC constructed four lean-tos, picnic tables, a ranger's cabin, and a dam across the stream. This became the park's Katahdin Stream Campground. (Courtesy Special Collections Department, Raymond H. Fogler Library, University of Maine, Bert Call Collection.)

Foster Field along the Sourdnahunk-Millinocket Tote Road was an extensive lumber camp before it became a CCC camp in the mid-1930s for those working southwest of Katahdin. Shown here is a CCC building with the sharp twin peaks of Doubletop Mountain in the center and Moose Mountain to the left. (Courtesy Acadia National Park, William Otis Sawtelle Center.)

Though there were rough lean-tos and cabins built at Chimney Pond earlier, the state of Maine built this more substantial cabin in 1924 to provide for the game warden assigned there for the summer. Roy Dudley was named to that position and lived there until his untimely death in 1942. (Courtesy Special Collections Department, Raymond H. Fogler Library, University of Maine, Bert Call Collection.)

Prior to the building of the state cabin at Chimney Pond, Roy Dudley, the future game warden, often stayed in this rough-hewn lean-to he built. It was called Dudley's Den by his friends. Of note is the rustic cooking area along with pots and pans. (Courtesy Special Collections Department, Raymond H. Fogler Library, University of Maine, Bert Call Collection.)

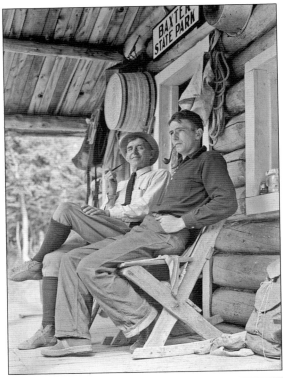

The porch of the state cabin at Chimney Pond became the center of activity at this remote and beautiful campsite at the foot of Katahdin's great glacial cirque. Here, Dudley relaxes with a friend, likely at the end of a busy day. Of note are the sign over the door and Dudley's ever-present pipe. (Courtesy Special Collections Department, Raymond H. Fogler Library, University of Maine, Bert Call Collection.)

Roy Dudley was widely known for telling stories about his friendship with the mountain deity named Pamola. Campers gathered many evenings at the edge of Chimney Pond and sat entranced hearing of Roy's escapades with his unconventional friend. Many of the stories have been preserved and published. (Courtesy Special Collections Department, Raymond H. Fogler Library, University of Maine, Ralph Palmer Collection.)

There are no marked trails up the steep headwall to the peaks along the Knife Edge. The Chimney Trail, no longer in use, ascended a rocky dry wash and can be traced in this photograph. (Courtesy Special Collections Department, Raymond H. Fogler Library, University of Maine, Bert Call Collection.)

Here, Roy Dudley, state game warden at Chimney Pond, is resting during an ascent of the Chimney Trail toward Pamola and Chimney Peaks. There were likely a number of occasions when Dudley had to rescue inexperienced climbers who got stuck at one of the notorious chockstones blocking the trail. (Courtesy Special Collections Department, Raymond H. Fogler Library, University of Maine, Bert Call Collection.)

Widely agreed as the most exciting climb on Katahdin, the one-mile Knife Edge between the summit and Pamola Peak is a narrow mass of jumbled rock with remarkable views of the countryside below. Here, a group is approaching South Peak on its way to the summit. Beyond the ridge is Katahdin Lake. (Courtesy the family of Frank T. Knaut.)

This old photograph shows hikers viewing the famous Knife Edge. Gov. Percival Baxter "crawled" across this glacial ridge in 1920 on his first ascent of Katahdin. That experience led him to a lifetime commitment to protect the area for all people looking for a wilderness experience in the north woods. (Courtesy Maine State Archives.)

This young man, having reached Baxter Peak, is resting on the summit cairn and recording his feat by snapping pictures with his faithful collapsible Kodak camera. The cameras of bygone days did a remarkable job of recording the wonders of the Katahdin area. This volume is evidence of that. (Courtesy Special Collections Department, Raymond H. Fogler Library, University of Maine, Bert Call Collection.)

Not far below Pamola Peak along the Dudley Trail is this glacial erratic rock aptly named Index Rock. Though it is a challenge to clamor to its sharp peak, it makes for a fine picture and a break from the rigors of the trail. In the background is the Traveler with the shoulder of North Turner on the right. (Courtesy Maine State Archives.)

This is the view from the rim of the North Basin looking back to the Great Basin and the Knife Edge with Hamlin Ridge in the foreground. The North Basin is well known for its abundance of blueberries and views east toward the Turners and Katahdin Lake. (Courtesy the estate of Paul A. Knaut Jr.)

Just below the tree line throughout Baxter State Park, the hardy spruce and fir are stunted by force of wind, ice, and snow, causing the small branches to remain close to the surface to survive. The result is an intertwined, jumbled growth of *krummholz*, which is extremely difficult to cross, as this group is finding. (Courtesy Maine Appalachian Trail Club, Avery Scrapbook.)

The Northwest Basin is a remote region with only one overnight lean-to at the edge of a pond below the glacial cirque. Here, a group traverses a low ridge full of sheep laurel; they appear to be picking blueberries. Some early visitors to the basin reported hearing night voices from the steep cliffs that surround the pond. (Courtesy Appalachian Mountain Club Library and Archives.)

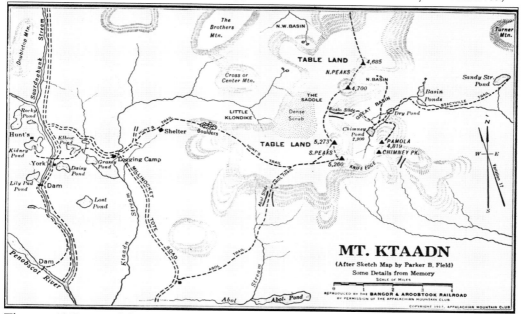

This is a 1917 map of the Katahdin area provided by the Appalachian Mountain Club for the Bangor & Aroostook Railroad's annual publication *In the Maine Woods*. It helped early visitors to find their way around before detailed trail maps were developed. The map features the old spelling of the mountain's name—*Ktaadn*. (Courtesy Appalachian Mountain Club Library and Archives.)

The ranger's cabin at Katahdin Stream Campground is a center of activity for AT hikers arriving to finish or begin their 2,000-mile trek along the spine of the Appalachians. Here, the log/register is kept for the thru-hikers who visit. (Courtesy Special Collections Department, Raymond H. Fogler Library, University of Maine, Bert Call Collection.)

Observing the abundance of flora found in the Katahdin region is one of the joys of hiking there. Mushrooms and a variety of ground cover are found along the trails and in the woods beyond. Their presence reminds us that all nature shares this wilderness area, and it must be respected and preserved. (Courtesy John W. Neff.)

Just below the tree line on the Hunt Trail, this huge boulder offers sanctuary to the climber. At one time, hikers were allowed to camp overnight there on their way to the summit. Here, Irving O. Hunt (right), who first cut the Hunt Trail from his Kidney Pond Camps, is with a companion at "the cave." (Courtesy Tony York.)

Here, a group of men are cooking their dinner and will be spending the night at "the cave" along the Hunt Trail on the way to the summit. Camping at any location other than park campgrounds or designated remote wilderness sites is now prohibited. (Courtesy Specials Collections Department, Raymond H. Fogler Library, University of Maine, Bert Call Collection.)

These hikers are looking from the Hunt Trail across Witherle Ravine to the southern face of The Owl. The Owl rewards those who climb it with a unique perspective of Katahdin and a bird's-eye view of the expanse of the inaccessible Klondike. (Courtesy Special Collections Department, Raymond H. Fogler Library, University of Maine, Bert Call Collection.)

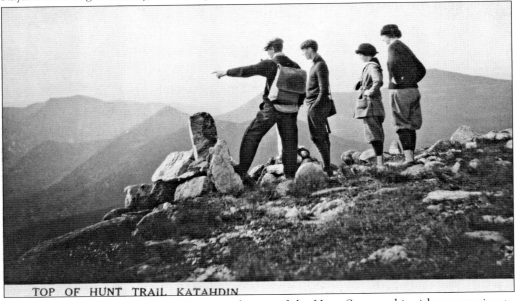

TOP OF HUNT TRAIL KATAHDIN

The same party has reached the Gateway, the top of the Hunt Spur, and is either preparing to ascend the gradual slope of the Tableland to the summit or descend to the Katahdin Stream Campground. This vista affords hikers spectacular views of both Chesuncook and Chamberlain Lakes. (Courtesy Maine Historic Preservation Commission.)

In 1816, the Abol Slide, a great avalanche, roared down the south side of Katahdin. As climbers descend the trail from the Tableland, they must first go through a series of huge boulders before reaching the loose rock of the slide. Here, one such boulder area is known as the Eye of the Needle. (Courtesy Maine Historic Preservation Commission.)

Here, Charlotte Millet (right) and Emmie Whitney ascend through the Abol Trail boulders on their way to the Tableland. Most of the early explorers to the Katahdin region climbed the mountain by way of this avalanche. It was easily seen and reached from the Penobscot West Branch. (Courtesy Collections of the Maine Historical Society, Maine Memory Network.)

The intrepid climbers who appear on the cover of this volume are shown having a lunch break during their ascent of the Abol Slide. The jumbled mass of rock created by the great avalanche of 1816 is visible. (Courtesy Special Collections Department, Raymond H. Fogler Library, University of Maine, Bert Call Collection.)

After the above party reached the Tableland and crossed to the summit, they began their descent. Here, later in the day as the shadows lengthened, they are looking out over the countryside before hastening down the trail to their campsite. (Courtesy Special Collections Department, Raymond H. Fogler Library, University of Maine, Bert Call Collection.)

This 1939 photograph shows Myron H. Avery, president of the Maine Appalachian Trail Club, on Sentinel Mountain pointing out features of the Katahdin region in the distance to an Appalachian Trail Conference group. Avery was instrumental in constructing the AT across Maine. Sentinel is not far from Kidney Pond. (Courtesy Maine State Library, Avery Collection.)

Crews through the years have maintained and improved the trails throughout Baxter State Park. These young men and women have worked hard and rendered great service in preserving the integrity of the trail system. Their work continues to this day, an effort much appreciated by all who use the pathways. (Courtesy Baxter State Park.)

Ronald Gower, longtime member and officer of the Appalachian Mountain Club, is shown here repainting a sign to Russell Pond Campground in the interior backcountry of the park. Gower and members of the club were avid trail maintainers until the park was able to shoulder those responsibilities after World War II. (Courtesy Appalachian Mountain Club Library and Archives.)

To provide safe crossing of the South Branch of Wassataquoik Stream, a cable system was rigged up in the early 1960s to carry hikers and packs across. This hiker is being pulled across by cable from the bank of the stream. It was a daunting experience and later proved inadequate as trail use increased. (Courtesy Charlotte Hall Kirkpatrick.)

Russell Pond Camps were established by William Tracy in the mid-1920s to bring people inland from the Penobscot East Branch for fishing and hunting. He continued to improve the site and once erected a sign that read, "Trout Limit—25 a day." He later cut a trail to the lumber road at Roaring Brook. (Courtesy Maine State Library, Baxter Collection.)

The Russell Pond Camps expanded to include a home for the Tracys, a shed for equipment, and cabins for guests. The pond was and still is a favorite gathering place for moose and other wildlife. From the north end, there are spectacular views of North and South Turner Mountains. (Courtesy Maine State Library, Baxter Collection.)

The Russell Pond Camps were the only sporting camps in the Katahdin region to remain under one owner (Bill Tracy) throughout their whole existence. After ownership passed to Percival Baxter in 1941, the site became a park campground in 1950. Its first ranger, Ralph Dolley, is shown constructing a lean-to. (Courtesy Baxter State Park.)

Ralph Dolley remained the ranger at Russell Ponds Camps for 10 years and was responsible for cutting new trails in the region and developing the site. The campground still requires a rigorous day's backpack to reach, but the experience there is worth the effort. Here, Dolley is looking out over the pond toward North Turner Mountain. (Courtesy Baxter State Park.)

Located four miles from Russell Pond Campground, the remote Wassataquoik Lake provides a single island lean-to for the visitor, the use of a canoe, and the memory of being alone overnight in a wilderness area. This view, from the scree slope of South Pogy Mountain, shows the long, narrow island and the Wassataquoik Valley beyond. (Courtesy John W. Neff.)

Before an open-front lean-to was built recently on the island in Wassataquoik Lake, a simple cabin provided accommodation. The cabin had a canvas roof that was removed for the winter, but a later renovation included a shingled roof. A special experience is to walk to the end of the long, slender island at sunset. (Courtesy Patten Lumbermen's Museum.)

At the outlet of Wassataquoik Lake, remains of an old sluice dam could be seen until recent years. Logs were stored on the lake until spring when they were sluiced through the dam and floated toward Wassataquoik Stream and the Penobscot East Branch. (Courtesy Special Collections Department, Raymond H. Fogler Library, University of Maine, Harold Dyer Collection.)

The responsibilities of Maine's game wardens required them to roam remote areas of the Katahdin region to be sure the laws of the state were observed by sportsmen and trappers. This cabin at Town Line Brook was typical of the rugged accommodations encountered during their forays into wilderness areas. (Courtesy Maine State Library, Baxter Collection.)

The seething waters of Grand Falls Wassataquoik are at the end of a popular trail from Russell Pond Campground. The cascade was a major impediment for loggers trying to run logs toward the Penobscot East Branch. A dynamited diversion helped at one time, but the watercourse has returned to its former path. (Courtesy Maine State Library, Baxter Collection.)

Nestled at the base of a small headwall, Twin Ponds are on the eastern side of North and South Turner Mountains. Here, Ranger Ed Werler dresses fish caught in the larger pond in the 1950s. A new park trail from Katahdin Lake has opened these remote mountain ponds to day hikers. (Courtesy Charlotte Hall Kirkpatrick.)

The northern part of Baxter State Park includes a major portion of Grand Lake Matagamon, headwaters of the Penobscot East Branch. Dams erected at its outlet kept water levels high for both logging operations and recreational use. Shown is one of the earliest dams near the northern gate into the park. (Courtesy Patten Lumbermen's Museum.)

The northern part of Baxter State Park was logged heavily in the early 20th century by the Eastern Corporation. A huge load of logs on a sled in the Trout Brook area is being prepared here for transportation to a stream or river for the spring river drive. (Courtesy Maine State Library, Avery Collection.)

Here, a fisherman is casting his line into Grand Lake Matagamon with Horse Mountain rising sharply in the background. The location is quite near the outlet dam where the waters of the lake become the Penobscot East Branch. In this northeastern corner of Baxter State Park, there is a network of trails into Billfish, Long, and Lower and Middle Fowler Ponds. (Courtesy Charlotte Hall Kirkpatrick.)

To provide for the lumbermen and animals working in the woods in the northern part of what would become Baxter State Park, a large farm along Trout Brook was established in the late 19th century. The site, purchased by Governor Baxter in the mid-1950s, was developed as the Trout Brook Farm Campground. It is a favorite of those wishing to reach nearby backcountry campsites. (Courtesy, Maine State Library, Avery Collection.)

Webster Stream flows out of Webster Lake, allowing canoeists to reach the Penobscot East Branch from the Allagash region of northern Maine. Henry David Thoreau followed this route in 1857 when he canoed to Grand Lake Matagamon and camped near this cascade. There is a park campsite not far below Grand Pitch shown here. (Courtesy Charlotte Hall Kirkpatrick.)

During his three trips to the north Maine woods, Thoreau was intrigued by the flora and fauna he saw. He kept detailed notes of his observations along the way. The mushroom and other plants, some very rare, abound throughout Baxter State Park from the alpine regions to the backcountry extending to the north. (Courtesy Charlotte Hall Kirkpatrick.)

South Branch Pond is one of the gems of the park. It offers campsites in a remote, seldom visited area. Visitors may climb the rigorous Traveler Loop, explore the wonders of Howe Brook, fish the waters for native eastern brook trout, and investigate the area's rich geological history. (Courtesy the estate of Paul A. Knaut Jr.)

The steep precipitous cliffs of Upper South Branch Pond reward the paddler who ventures there with a stunning view of the high terrain that surrounds this remote mountain tarn. Backpackers seeking to reach the interior backcountry at Russell Pond may pass along the shore, and hawks may be seen circling the cliffs. (Courtesy Charlotte Hall Kirkpatrick.)

When exploring the Baxter State Park backcountry, visitors are likely to come across evidence of thriving beaver populations. This giant hardwood was cut over a considerable period of time—but the persistent beaver eventually won the battle, and the tree fell. Lester Hall examines the beaver's work at water's edge. (Courtesy Charlotte Hall Kirkpatrick.)

The steep, tumbling waters of Howe Brook offer a trip back in geologic time. Potholes and sluices have been carved in the rock over the centuries. A major waterfall descends sharply into a dark ravine. At the mouth of the brook, visitors are mystified as the waters disappear and flow underground into Lower South Branch Pond. (Courtesy Charlotte Hall Kirkpatrick.)

Camp Natarswi, a Girl Scout camp located on Lower Togue Pond, is blessed with a spectacular view of Katahdin. The camp was founded in the 1930s on a 30-acre site vacated by the CCC, and when the Togue Pond parcel was acquired by Baxter State Park, the property became an inholding. (Courtesy Special Collections Department, Raymond H. Fogler Library, University of Maine, Bert Call Collection.)

Here, a young woman walks in the sylvan setting of the Appalachian Trail. In the mid-1930s, Camp Natarswi was among the first summer camps in the state to take advantage of the camping and hiking opportunities afforded by the new park. (Courtesy Special Collections Department, Raymond H. Fogler Library, University of Maine, Bert Call Collection.)

Camp Chewonki did not routinely send youngsters to Katahdin until the 1950s. This photograph and the three that follow are from the camp's inaugural trip in 1950. This obligatory "departure photograph" was taken on-site in Wiscasset, Maine. Half a century later, Chewonki acquired the Big Eddy Campground on the Penobscot West Branch. (Courtesy Gordon Hall.)

In addition to the summit climb, the Chewonki trip included backpacking to Russell Pond from Roaring Brook. Here, several campers are seen rock hopping across a relatively low Wassataquoik Stream. This scene has been repeated over the years by backpackers, although pack baskets and wooden pack frames are seldom seen today. (Courtesy Gordon Hall.)

This campsite at Russell Pond is a relic of the mid-20th century with its oversized Adirondack lean-to and huge boulder cook fire. Nevertheless, it is well appointed with shelving and a hand-hewn table. On the return trip to Roaring Brook, buildings were seen still standing at the old New City Lumber Camp; however, the door lintels had rotted down to four feet. (Courtesy Gordon Hall.)

The Chewonki campers crossed the Knife Edge from Pamola Peak in less-than-ideal weather. Here, the group approaches South Peak enshrouded in clouds. Climbers should always consult weather forecasts before departing the trailhead, and once on the mountain, they should avoid crossing the Knife Edge in threatening weather. (Courtesy Gordon Hall.)

This 1925 photograph shows three climbers in the Chimney. The park affords winter campers with a variety of options, including snowshoeing, skiing, and winter mountain hiking and climbing. A park ranger is assigned to Chimney Pond during the winter camping season. However, the park states unequivocally that all winter backcountry users are personally responsible for their safety. (Courtesy Maine State Library, Avery Collection.)

In December 1974, the Adirondack Mountain Club and the Appalachian Mountain Club sponsored an advanced mountaineering school at Katahdin. The post-school report indicated that the weather was nearly perfect, as seen in this photograph, and most of the students climbed Baxter Peak via the Chimney and the Knife Edge. (Courtesy William Bentley.)

Mountaineering school instructor William Bentley is shown here on an ice face. Baxter State Park provides a comprehensive winter-use handbook designed to assist visitors in planning trips, promoting safety, and preventing unnecessary search-and-rescue efforts. (Courtesy William Bentley.)

Here, four members of the mountaineering group stand facing the fog-shrouded headwall of the South Basin. In 2010, Baxter State Park's revision of its winter-use policies met with a swift, positive response from the winter camping and climbing community. (Courtesy William Bentley.)

In the mid- to late 1930s, area forest ranger Jack Grant began to haul gear by horseback for clients heading to Chimney Pond. The horses could even follow the trail on their own. Later, in the 1950s, park ranger Ed Werler continued the popular service using burros. Here, Ed is ascending the Chimney Pond Trail. (Courtesy Appalachian Mountain Club Library and Archives.)

When Ed Werler corralled his burros in the morning for the trip from Chimney Pond to Roaring Brook, it was a festive moment at the campground. Here, the gear is being loaded onto the burro train before heading down the steep, rocky trail. Nancy, one of Ed's burros, lived to the ripe old age of 40 years. (Courtesy Maine State Library, Avery Collection.)

Packhorse expeditions took place in the Katahdin region before the founding of the park in the 1930s. Here, a group (possibly in the early 1900s) has paused along the old Appalachian Trail leading from Chimney Pond to Basin Ponds. The lower slopes of Pamola Peak are visible in the background, and the walls of the South Basin appear in the upper-right-hand corner. (Courtesy Appalachian Mountain Club Library and Archives.)

Moose abound in Baxter State Park, and visitors must always be on the lookout for these huge, powerful monarchs of the north woods. There are a number of places in the park where moose will likely be found. They most commonly feed on aquatic plants in the ponds and lakes in the region. (Courtesy Baxter State Park.)

Governor Baxter's strong commitment to sustainable land management was manifested by his decision in 1955 to set aside nearly 30,000 acres in the northwestern corner of the park for the practice of scientific forestry. It was his hope that the Scientific Forestry Management Area (SFMA) would become a model forest similar to those in Europe. (Courtesy Baxter State Park.)

Jensen Bissell's appointment as resource manager of the SFMA in 1987 marked a turning point in achieving the model scientific forestry practices envisioned by Baxter. After nearly two decades with the forestry program, Bissell was appointed director of Baxter State Park in 2005. Here, he is shown in his former capacity with the SFMA. (Courtesy Baxter State Park.)

Here, a logger in the SFMA is operating the single-grip, fixed-head processor. The processor has three tasks: to fell the tree, de-limb the stem, and cut the stem into desired lengths. The harvested trees are de-limbed in the woods so the slash and associated nutrients stay on-site to reduce ground compaction and soil damage. (Courtesy William Bentley.)

The forwarder moves the cut logs from the woods to the roadside and sorts them into different piles based on their destination and product type, such as saw logs or pulp. The forwarder is more than able to keep up with the processor and therefore hauls less-than capacity loads, thereby reducing further soil damage. (Courtesy William Bentley.)

As a young man, US Supreme Court justice William O. Douglas regularly visited the Kidney Pond Camps operated by Roy Bradeen. He returned with "Jake's Rangers" in the fall of 1959 when he was writing his classic *My Wilderness: East to Katahdin* (1961). Douglas said, "We must multiply the Baxter Parks a thousandfold." (Courtesy Collections of Baxter State Park, Maine Memory Network.)

This expansive view of the Tableland and the Hunt Trail is a reminder that glaciers put the finishing touches on the mountain landscape. Those interested in the bedrock and surficial geology should consult Douglas W. Rankin and Dabney W. Caldwell's *A Guide to the Geology of Baxter State Park and Katahdin* (2010). (Courtesy Special Collections Department, Raymond H. Fogler Library, University of Maine, Bert Call Collection.)

Percival Baxter's views regarding automobile traffic on the Tote Road are legendary. In 1957, he wrote state highway commissioner David H. Stevens, "I find that those who visit the park do not mind the crooked roads or the many turn-outs; in fact these give a little zest to the journey." (Courtesy Special Collections Department, Raymond H. Fogler Library, University of Maine, Harold Dyer Collection.)

The beaver, a large semi-aquatic rodent, finds the habitat in the park ideal for building its dams, canals, and lodges. This large beaver lodge is on Sandy Stream with South Turner Mountain in the distance. The prevalence of beavers in park waters compounds the risk of the waterborne Giardia disease. (Courtesy Acadia National Park, William Otis Sawtelle Center.)

It might take a moment for someone familiar with Baxter State Park to identify the location of this image. The campers' tent site is on the far shore of Chimney Pond looking toward Hamlin Ridge. This type of impromptu camping at unauthorized sites is prohibited by park regulations. (Courtesy Special Collections Department, Raymond H. Fogler Library, University of Maine, Bert Call Collection.)

This "Cut No Green Trees" sign dates from a period well before the "Leave No Trace" practices of today's environmentally conscious campers. Here, Roy Dudley with his ever-present pipe is engaged in informal conversation with a group of campers at a Chimney Pond lean-to. (Courtesy Special Collections Department, Raymond H. Fogler Library, University of Maine, Bert Call Collection.)

This sign near the shore of Chimney Pond informs hikers and campers that bathing or washing dishes is prohibited. The use of soap or detergent or the disposal of food scraps in the streams or waters of the park is prohibited. All garbage and trash must be carried out. (Courtesy Maine State Library, Avery Collection.)

The widespread existence of waterborne diseases, such as Giardia, necessitates that all water used for drinking and preparation of food should be purified. Campers and hikers have an array of options available to them to ensure their safety from waterborne diseases. (Courtesy Special Collections Department, Raymond H. Fogler Library, University of Maine, Bert Call Collection.)

Artist Jake Day, of Damariscotta, visited the park frequently, and in the 1960s, he began leading a group of men from his hometown. They became known as Jake's Rangers and were even called upon to lead US Supreme Court justice William O. Douglas (second from right) on two trips to the park in 1959 and 1960. (Courtesy Baxter State Park.)

Artist Jake Day is sketching at one of his favorite places in the park near Russell Pond. He and his friend Lester Hall, of Nobleboro, began visiting the park in the early 1930s and explored the area before there were many roads and trails, especially into remote areas. (Courtesy Collections of Baxter State Park, Maine Memory Network.)

Whitetail deer abound in the park and are often seen along the trails. Katahdin deer became models for the memorable animated movie *Bambi* in the late 1930s when Maine artist Jake Day, at that time a Walt Disney Studios employee, was sent back to Maine to do the original sketches for the movie. (Courtesy Baxter State Park.)

This picture was taken by artist Jake Day to show the field at the foot of Russell Mountain that inspired his *Bambi* movie drawings of the meadow where the woodland creatures gathered and sought protection from dangers lurking nearby. It was the site of the New City Lumber Camp. (Courtesy Charlotte Hall Kirkpatrick.)

Photography in the Katahdin region goes back to the 1860s when photographers accompanied canoe adventurers. Here, renowned photographer Bert Call, or his assistant, sets up a tripod and camera early in the 20th century for a shot of the headwall of the South Basin at Chimney Pond. (Courtesy Special Collections Department, Raymond H. Fogler Library, University of Maine, Bert Call Collections.)

Here, a Katahdin climber looks from huge boulders to the distant vista of the saddle between Katahdin and Hamlin Peak. Beyond the saddle stretches the Northwest Plateau leading to the remote Klondike and the Northwest Basin. (Courtesy Special Collections Department, Raymond H. Fogler Library, University of Maine, Bert Call Collection.)

This image of the Tableland with its dense *krummholz* shows where 12-year-old Donn Fendler wandered aimlessly as evening approached after being separated in a storm from his companion. Fendler's story *Lost on a Mountain in Maine* (1939) is a classic still widely read among schoolchildren and adults in Maine and elsewhere. (Courtesy Special Collections Department, Raymond H. Fogler Library, University of Maine, Ralph Palmer Collection.)

An extraordinary July 25, 1939, entry in Dudley's Chimney Pond ledger book reports "lost boy" (Donn Fendler) had been found alive along the Penobscot East Branch. Fendler was found upriver from Hunt Farm across from the Lunksoos Camps. The volume also records the names of the nearly 200 men who participated in the search that had begun on the night of July 17. (Courtesy Baxter State Park.)

In the summer of 1940, a year after his ordeal on the mountain, Donn Fendler returned to the park and visited the legendary Roy Dudley at Chimney Pond. Fendler would go on to a distinguished military career in both the Korean and Vietnam conflicts. (Courtesy Donn Fendler.)

In 1974, a group of six accomplished mountaineers was forced to bivouac above the tree line on Pamola in a fierce winter storm. One of the mountaineers died from hypothermia, and others were seriously injured. When the weather permitted a number of days later, a search-and-rescue team is seen preparing to place the victim aboard a National Guard helicopter atop Pamola Peak. (Courtesy Baxter State Park.)

In 1912, the Maine Forest Service established a fire lookout station near the top of the Abol Slide. Frank Sewall was assigned to the post and built a log cabin on the site in 1913. Persistent clouds and mist made spotting fires difficult, and the service was discontinued in 1919. (Courtesy Special Collections Department, Raymond H. Fogler Library, University of Maine, Bert Call Collection.)

Frank Sewall stands in front of his cabin just off the Abol Slide where he lived while on fire-lookout duty. The tote road from Millinocket enabled him to bring in his weekly supplies and backpack them to the cabin. (Courtesy Special Collections Department, Raymond H. Fogler Library, University of Maine, Bert Call Collection.)

In 1932, a major storm hit the Katahdin area causing flood and wind damage throughout the region. The toll dam on Nesowadnehunk Stream (shown here) was badly damaged and never fully repaired. The storm also caused new slides to come down on OJI Mountain. (Courtesy Maine State Library, Avery Collection.)

The 1932 storm damaged many streams around Katahdin. Game warden Roy Dudley was marooned at Chimney Pond for a number of days when waters off the mountain overran the normal flowage patterns, leaving the campground isolated for a time. Damage to Avalanche Brook (shown here) was considerable. (Courtesy Collections of Maine Historical Society, Maine Memory Network.)

Devastating forest fires have always plagued the remote Katahdin area. This 3,500-acre fire broke out in July 1977 along the Penobscot West Branch. Of note is how close the fire approached the slopes of the mountain. The absence of old growth can still be observed along the Tote Road in the Abol/Katahdin Stream areas. (Courtesy Collections of Baxter State Park, Maine Memory Network.)

The 1977 forest fire was fueled by debris from an enormous windstorm that blew down trees three years earlier southwest of Katahdin. Parts of the Appalachian Trail within the park were affected but were restored by members of the Maine Appalachian Trail Club the next year. (Courtesy Collections of Baxter State Park, Maine Memory Network.)

Towers were erected for fire detection in the Katahdin area early in the 20th century. Erected in 1913, this tower on Doubletop Mountain enabled the spotter to see a vast area from Katahdin to the Moosehead region and south toward the sea. (Courtesy Special Collections Department, Raymond H. Fogler Library, University of Maine, Bert Call Collection.)

Fires even occurred close to Katahdin's tree line. This picture taken from near Basin Ponds shows damage from minor fires that broke out in 1923 and in the early 1930s. Katahdin Lake is in the distance. The forest takes much longer to recover in these fragile areas. (Courtesy Special Collections Department, Raymond H. Fogler Library, University of Maine, Bert Call Collection.)

Four

WILDERNESS CHALLENGED AND DEFENDED

Governor Baxter embedded the phrase, "shall forever be left in the natural wild state" in most of the deeds of trust he used to convey land to the state. This mandate has from time to time been challenged by those who wish the park to be more accessible to a greater variety of recreational uses. The wilderness character of the park has, however, been successfully defended time and again. In addition to this legal mandate, the wilderness qualities of this special place have been sustained by devoted citizen advocates, the founding of Friends of Baxter State Park, and the solid support of park staff.

The last photograph found in Chapter Three shows the devastation of the land caused by unregulated logging and the resulting increased threat of fires. The image is representative of the situation before stewardship of the wild character of the area was in effect. In contrast, a series of photographs in this chapter shows the park today with its wilderness values intact and strengthening with each passing year. As said at the beginning, the human and cultural history of the region is a significant part of what makes this place so remarkable.

The American Wilderness Act of 1964 declared that wilderness is where the community of life is untrammeled by human presence, where we are only visitors who do not remain, and where there are outstanding opportunities for solitude and primitive recreation. The mission of Baxter State Park is to remain faithful to those values, which are so important to the welfare of the human family, and to provide one of those places where visitors' inner soul energy can be renewed. This must not be merely Governor Baxter's vision: it must be shared by everyone who loves the wilderness places of the earth.

Residents and visitors alike in the small communities along the park's eastern boundary have always been blessed with an expansive view of the Katahdin range as it trends due north from the massif to the Travelers. This photograph of Katahdin's east-facing glacial basins was taken from Patten's Ash Hill on a brilliant sunny, subzero January day. (Courtesy William Bentley.)

Ever since the first recorded visit to the South Basin in 1847, Chimney Pond has played an integral role in Katahdin's history. In 1924, the state of Maine's presence was established with the construction of a "State Cabin" for its resident game warden Roy Dudley. Today, Chimney Pond Campground affords hikers with an exquisite view of the basin's cirque and several trails to Baxter Peak. (Courtesy William Bentley.)

A short distance from the southwest shore of Wassataquoik Lake, visitors can climb briefly to the remote Greene Falls. As they watch the waters cascade over the moss-covered face of the falls, they are easily transported back to when the area was an undisturbed wilderness. The falls were named for either a logging-era boss or Walter Greene, who helped build and mark the Appalachian Trail in Maine in the 1930s. (Courtesy William Bentley.)

The most remote and least visited of Katahdin's major glacial basins is found nestled between the Klondike and the North Peaks. Since the end of the logging era, Davis Pond in the Northwest Basin has been the site of either a mountain hut or an Adirondack lean-to, a much-coveted overnight destination for those seeking a solitary wilderness experience. (Courtesy William Bentley.)

Webster Brook flows out of Webster Lake in the far northern area of Baxter State Park. After eight miles, the stream explodes across Grand Pitch falls, soon entering the waters of Grand Lake Matagamon. A park trail follows the course of the brook and the lake and provides an unparalleled remote backcountry experience. Henry David Thoreau came this way in July 1857 and camped near the falls. (Courtesy William Bentley.)

Trails in the northern sector of Baxter State Park offer more remote yet still challenging hikes. For many years, visitors could climb North Traveler on one trail and Traveler Mountain on another but could not climb from one to the other at high elevation. That was finally remedied when a connecting trail was built recently, creating the challenging but spectacular Traveler Loop. Seen here is but a taste of that experience. (Courtesy William Bentley.)

The Knife Edge at the head of South Basin's cirque provides hikers with the most spectacular and potentially dangerous terrain on Katahdin. A mile-long trail across the narrow, saw-tooth ridge extends from Baxter Peak to Pamola. In 1920, Percival Baxter "crept gingerly over the rough piles of loose and broken rock," unashamedly availing himself of the "friendly and reassuring hand" of his companion. (Courtesy William Bentley.)

Katahdin Lake was an integral part of Baxter's designs for a park at Katahdin as early as 1921; however, he was unable to acquire it from Great Northern Paper Company during his lifetime. In 2006, the state of Maine with the assistance of the Trust for Public Land negotiated a complex land swap, and the 649-acre lake and surrounding lands became part of Baxter State Park. (Courtesy William Bentley.)

BIBLIOGRAPHY

Austin, Phyllis. *Wilderness Partners: Buzz Caverly and Baxter State Park*. Gardiner, ME: Tilbury House, 2008.

Baxter State Park: Mount Katahdin/Katahdin Iron Works, Maine, USA. Evergreen, CO: National Geographic Maps, 2011.

Bernbaum, Edwin. *Sacred Mountains of the World*. San Francisco, CA: Sierra Club Books, 1990.

Clark, Stephen. *Katahdin: A Guide to Baxter State Park and Katahdin*. 6th ed. Shapleigh, ME: Clark Books, 2009. (Baxter State Park has acquired the copyright and will publish a new edition in 2012.)

Eckstorm, Fannie Hardy. *The Penobscot Man*. Boston: Houghton, Mifflin & Company, 1904.

Field, David B. *Along Maine's Appalachian Trail*. Charleston, SC: Arcadia Publishing, 2011.

Hakola, John W. *Legacy of a Lifetime: The Story of Baxter State Park*. Woolwich, ME: TBW Books, 1981.

Hall, Clayton, and Jane Thomas. *Chimney Pond Tales: Yarns Told by Leroy Dudley*. Cumberland Center, ME: Pamola Press, 1991.

Hempstead, Alfred G. *The Penobscot Boom*. Self-published, 1975.

Huber, J. Parker. *The Wildest Country: A Guide to Thoreau's Maine*. 2nd ed. Boston: Appalachian Mountain Club Books, 2008.

Katahdin/Baxter State Park Trail Map. Portland, ME: Map Adventures, 2011.

Kirkpatrick, Charlotte Hall. *Katahdin Comrades, The Journals of Lester F. Hall*. Woolwich, ME: Self-published, 2010.

Leavitt, H. Walter. *Katahdin Skylines*. Orono, ME: University of Maine Press, 1954.

Neff, John W. *Katahdin: An Historic Journey*. Boston: Appalachian Mountain Club Books, 2006.

Percival P. Baxter's Vision for Baxter State Park: An Annotated Compilation of Original Sources. 4 vols. Annotated by Howard R. Whitcomb. Bangor, ME: Friends of Baxter State Park, 2005.

Rankin, Douglas, and Dabney W. Caldwell. *A Guide to the Geology of Baxter State Park and Katahdin*. Augusta, ME: Maine Geological Survey, 2010.

Rolde, Neil. *The Baxters of Maine: Downeast Visionaries*. Gardiner, ME: Tilbury House, 1997.

Scee, Trudy Irene. *In the Deeds We Trust: Baxter State Park, 1970–1994*. Standish, ME: Tower Publishing, 1999.

Thoreau, Henry David. *The Maine Woods*. Edited by Joseph J. Moldenhauer. Princeton, NJ: Princeton UP, 2004.

Whitcomb, Howard R. *Governor Baxter's Magnificent Obsession: A Documentary History of Baxter State Park, 1931–2006*. Bangor, ME: Friends of Baxter State Park, 2008.

Note: Excellent collections of the extensive literature of Baxter State Park and Katahdin can be found at the Bangor Public Library, Baxter State Park, Maine Historical Society, Maine State Library, and the University of Maine's Raymond H. Fogler Library.

ABOUT THE ORGANIZATIONS

BAXTER STATE PARK

Baxter State Park's mission is to carry out the wishes of the park's donor, Percival Baxter, as expressed in the Deeds of Gift and Formal Communication: to protect the natural resources of the park for the enjoyment of present and future generations; to provide various appropriate recreational opportunities to park visitors; to conduct exemplary sustainable forest management operations within the park's 29,537-acre Scientific Forest Management Area; to maintain facilities, infrastructure, and data systems of the park; to provide for the safety of park staff and visitors; and to manage and protect the fiscal integrity and independence of the park for current and future generations.

Baxter State Park
64 Balsam Drive
Millinocket, ME, 04462-2110
www.baxterstateparkauthority.com

FRIENDS OF BAXTER STATE PARK

Friends of Baxter State Park is an independent citizen group working to preserve, support, and enhance the wilderness character of Baxter State Park in the spirit of its founder, Gov. Percival Baxter.

Friends of Baxter State Park
P.O. Box 609
Union, ME, 04862-0609
www.friendsofbaxter.org

Discover Thousands of Local History Books
Featuring Millions of Vintage Images

Arcadia Publishing, the leading local history publisher in the United States, is committed to making history accessible and meaningful through publishing books that celebrate and preserve the heritage of America's people and places.

Find more books like this at
www.arcadiapublishing.com

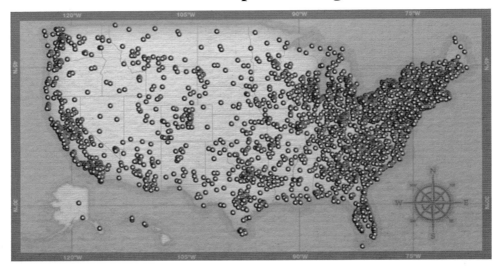

Search for your hometown history, your old stomping grounds, and even your favorite sports team.

Consistent with our mission to preserve history on a local level, this book was printed in South Carolina on American-made paper and manufactured entirely in the United States. Products carrying the accredited Forest Stewardship Council (FSC) label are printed on 100 percent FSC-certified paper.

MADE IN THE
USA